Here's all the great literature in this grade level of *Celebrate Reading!*

HARVEY,
the Foolish Pig

DICK GACKENBACH

BOOK A

Pig Tales

Stories That Twist

Miss Nelson Is Missing!
by Harry Allard
Illustrations by James Marshall
✳ CHILDREN'S CHOICE
✳ CALIFORNIA YOUNG READER MEDAL

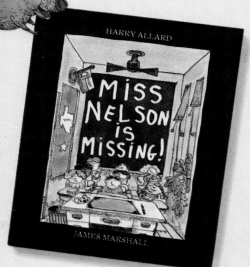

HARRY ALLARD

MISS NELSON IS MISSING!

JAMES MARSHALL

Harvey, the Foolish Pig
retold by Dick Gackenbach

King Wacky
by Dick Gackenbach
✳ CHILDREN'S CHOICE

Featured Poets

Jack Prelutsky
Arnold Lobel

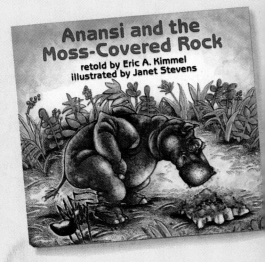

Anansi and the
Moss-Covered Rock
retold by Eric A. Kimmel
illustrated by Janet Stevens

Esmeralda and the Pet Parade
by Cecile Schoberle

**Anansi and the
Moss-Covered Rock**
retold by Eric A. Kimmel
Illustrations by Janet Stevens

Chicken Little
by Steven Kellogg
✳ CHILDREN'S CHOICE

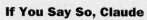

The BOY and the GHOST
by Robert D. San Souci / illustrated by J. Brian Pinkney

BOOK C

How Many Toes Does a Fish Have?

Looking Beneath the Surface

Featured Poet

Joan W. Blos

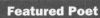
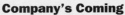

BOOK F

In Your Wildest Dreams

Imagination at Work

Featured Poets

A. A. Milne
Bill Peet

Celebrate Reading!
Trade Book Library

The Cactus Flower Bakery
by Harry Allard
✳ CHILDREN'S CHOICE AUTHOR

Play Ball, Amelia Bedelia
by Peggy Parish

Fables
by Arnold Lobel
✳ CALDECOTT MEDAL
✳ ALA NOTABLE BOOK

What's Cooking, Jenny Archer?
by Ellen Conford
✳ PARENTS' CHOICE AUTHOR

**She Come Bringing Me
That Little Baby Girl**
by Eloise Greenfield
✳ IRMA SIMONTON BLACK AWARD
✳ BOSTON GLOBE-HORN BOOK
   ILLUSTRATION HONOR
✳ CHILDREN'S CHOICE

The Show-and-Tell War
by Janice Lee Smith
✳ CHILDREN'S CHOICE
✳ SCHOOL LIBRARY JOURNAL BEST BOOK

King of the Birds
by Shirley Climo
✳ NOTABLE SOCIAL STUDIES TRADE BOOK

Fossils Tell of Long Ago
by Aliki
✳ LIBRARY OF CONGRESS
   CHILDREN'S BOOK
✳ OUTSTANDING SCIENCE TRADE BOOK

Willie's Not the Hugging Kind
by Joyce Durham Barrett

The Paper Crane
by Molly Bang
✳ ALA NOTABLE CHILDREN'S BOOK
✳ BOSTON GLOBE-HORN BOOK AWARD
✳ SCHOOL LIBRARY JOURNAL BEST BOOK
✳ READING RAINBOW SELECTION

Don't Tell the Whole World
by Joanna Cole
✳ CHILDREN'S CHOICE AUTHOR

**The Spooky Tail of
Prewitt Peacock**
by Bill Peet
✳ CHILDREN'S CHOICE AUTHOR

HOW MANY TOES DOES A FISH HAVE?

Looking Beneath the Surface

About the Cover Artist
Lisa Berrett lives in Northern California with her
husband, also an artist, and her Pug, Wally. She
has illustrated books for children as well as games,
puzzles, and educational materials.

ISBN 0-673-81141-7

1997
Scott, Foresman and Company, Glenview, Illinois
All Rights Reserved.
Printed in the United States of America.

Acknowledgments appear on page 128.

12345678910DQ010099989796

HOW MANY TOES DOES A FISH HAVE?

Looking Beneath the Surface

ScottForesman

A Division of HarperCollinsPublishers

Contents

Lucas Makes a Bet

by Johanna Hurwitz

One Thursday in November, Cricket Kaufman came rushing into the classroom all excited. "My mother had our baby," she announced very proudly to everyone.

"That's wonderful," said Mrs. Hockaday. "Is it a girl or a boy?"

"It's a girl baby," said Cricket. "And her name is Monica. My father says she looks just like me."

"How come they didn't name her after a bug like you?" asked Lucas. There were lots of names that he could think of: Mosquito Kaufman, Ladybug Kaufman, or Cockroach Kaufman.

Mrs. Hockaday ignored Lucas's comment. But Cricket surprised him by turning angrily and saying, "Oh yeah, well how come your parents didn't name you Mucus, to go with the names of your brothers—Marcus, Marius, and Mucus."

"Mucus!" Julio shouted. "Mucus Cott!"

"Julio. Stop that at once! You, too, Lucas. And I'm surprised at you, Cricket. You mustn't let Lucas's teasing make you so upset. If your sister grows up to be just like you, it will be a pleasure to have her in my class someday. But calling out is not proper behavior from anyone." She looked at Lucas and Julio sternly. "Is that understood?"

Lucas remembered that he had promised his mother he wasn't going to call out in class. But once again, he seemed to have forgotten. It seemed as if the words were always flying out of his mouth before he could remember to keep still. So now, even though he was furious at what Cricket had said, he kept quiet. He waited until they were walking out of class at the end of the day to tell her something he bet she didn't know.

"My name is Roman," he said. "And Marcus and Marius have Roman names, too. That's because my grandparents came from Italy, and in the olden days Rome was the most important place in the world."

"Well, that doesn't make you so important now," said Cricket. "You think you are so special because you have twins at your house. I bet my sister is going to be smarter than your brothers. And she's prettier, too."

"Don't you say anything against my brothers. They're better than your baby sister any day," said Lucas angrily.

"You haven't even seen my sister," said Cricket, sticking her tongue out at Lucas.

"You'll see," said Lucas knowingly. "Babies aren't all that great. They make a lot of noise and they smell, too. And they take up a lot of your parents' time. At least Marcus and Marius are two years old; they can learn things from me."

"If you are teaching them to be just like you, then they're going to get into trouble all the time, just like you."

"Oh yeah?"

"Yeah. You couldn't keep quiet if your life depended on it," Cricket said to Lucas. "Your mouth is open all day long. I'm surprised you don't wake yourself up talking in your sleep."

"Listen," said Lucas. "Mouths are meant for talking. And eating," he added, licking his lips.

"You don't eat all day, and you shouldn't talk all day, either," said Cricket. "Poor Mrs. Hockaday has to listen to you talking constantly."

"I don't talk that much," said Lucas, defending himself. "And besides, if I wanted to, I could stop talking. It's just that I have a lot to say."

"I bet you couldn't keep quiet for more than two seconds."

"Want to bet?" asked Lucas.

"Sure," said Cricket.

"What do you want to bet?" asked Lucas.

"My grandma gave me a dollar last night because I was such a big girl with my new baby sister. I'll bet you that dollar that you couldn't go through a day at school without saying a single word."

"You're on," said Lucas. "Tomorrow my lips will be sealed."

"Okay. But if you talk at all, if you say one single word in school tomorrow, then you have to give *me* a dollar," warned Cricket.

"No sweat," said Lucas. He didn't have a dollar to

pay her, but he had no intention of losing the bet. It would be an easy way to earn a dollar, and he would show Cricket Kaufman that she didn't know everything. He could be quiet if he wanted to. He just never had wanted to before. And after he won the bet, he would talk twice as much the next day to get her really annoyed. It was a great plan.

The next morning, Lucas left home and started off to school. He wasn't sure at which point the bet began. Could he speak in the school yard? What about during recess and lunchtime? No matter. He wouldn't say a word all day. There was no way that he was going to lose this bet.

"Hi, Lucas," Cricket called out as she saw him approaching.

Lucas nodded to her but he did not say anything.

"Don't forget," said Cricket. "One word and you owe me a dollar."

Lucas nodded his head in agreement and went into the classroom. There was no sense in standing around outside if he couldn't speak to anyone.

After a few minutes the bell rang and all the students filed into the classroom. Mrs. Hockaday came in and sat down at her desk. At the beginning of the school year, she had called the attendance each morning. But now that she knew all her students, she merely looked around the room and could spot who was absent.

"One hundred percent attendance," she said, looking up and down the rows. "That's a fine way to end the week."

Lucas was just about to call out that the best way to end the week was to go home, when he remembered that he was not going to speak. He pressed his lips together and took out his arithmetic workbook. He paid close attention to everything that Mrs. Hockaday wrote on the chalkboard, and he shook his head when Julio poked him to say something.

"What's the matter?" whispered Julio, noticing the way Lucas was keeping his lips pressed together. "You feel like throwing up or something?"

Lucas shook his head and kept writing in his workbook. He wanted to tell Julio that school always made him feel sick, but he knew he couldn't even whisper without Cricket hearing him. He looked in her direction and saw that she was watching him closely.

"Cricket? Why aren't you doing your problems?" Mrs. Hockaday called out.

"I'm finished already," Cricket replied proudly.

"Well, go over them again," said the teacher. "We don't want any careless errors."

Cricket pretended to go over her arithmetic, but Lucas could see that she was still watching him. This was going to be a long day.

During social studies, Mrs. Hockaday asked the class which explorer discovered the Pacific Ocean. Lucas knew the answer but he did not raise his hand. He listened as the students tried to guess the answer.

"Columbus," said Julio.

"Marco Polo," said Sara Jane.

Cricket was waving her hand frantically. "I know. I know," she called out.

"Of course you know, Cricket," said Mrs. Hockaday, smiling at her star student. "But I want some of the other students to try and remember. We talked about this man yesterday. Here is a clue: his name starts with a *B*."

No one seemed to know the answer except Cricket and Lucas. But Lucas couldn't say it without losing the bet, and Mrs. Hockaday didn't want to call on Cricket. She had already answered the last five questions that the teacher asked.

"Open your books to page seventy-two," Mrs. Hockaday instructed the class.

Everyone did.

"Now, Lucas, please start reading from the top of the page. You will find the answer to the question there."

Lucas froze. He looked over at Cricket. Did reading count as speaking? It had been stupid of him not to make the rules for this bet clear before he agreed to it.

Cricket was grinning from ear to ear. It was obvious to Lucas that she thought he would have to pay her a dollar if he read aloud in class. Lucas sat staring at page seventy-two, but he did not begin reading.

"Lucas," said Mrs. Hockaday, "we're all waiting."

Lucas thought fast. He began to cough. Then he doubled up and coughed into his hands.

"You had better get yourself a drink of water," Mrs. Hockaday said. "Julio, would you read from the top of page seventy-two?"

Lucas dashed out into the hall. He was lucky to have gotten out of that situation. He hoped he could keep it up through the rest of the day. He took a long, slow drink of water at the fountain and went back into the classroom.

"So now we all know who discovered the Pacific Ocean," Mrs. Hockaday was saying as he entered the classroom. "Lucas, do you know?" she asked.

Lucas stopped midway to his seat. He nodded his head and smiled at the teacher.

"Who was it?" asked Mrs. Hockaday.

Lucas was about to double up in a second coughing fit. However, he suddenly realized that he had another alternative. He walked to the front of the room and picked up a piece of chalk. BALBOA, he wrote on the chalkboard in huge letters.

"Excellent," said Mrs. Hockaday. "I'm glad to see that you know how to spell the name."

Lucas returned to his seat, smiling at Cricket as he passed her desk.

Lunch was hard. But it could have been harder. Lucas chewed his sandwich very, very slowly. He took teeny-tiny bites and teeny-tiny sips from his container of milk.

"What's the matter? Are you mad at me?" Julio asked.

Lucas smiled his friendliest smile but didn't answer. He pointed to his sandwich and then took another bite.

"You've gone bananas," said Julio.

Lucas wanted to ask how you could go bananas while eating a tuna fish sandwich, but he resisted the temptation. Tomorrow when he had his prize dollar from Cricket he would buy Julio a candy bar or a pack of gum.

USSR was easy. Lucas read his book while his classmates read theirs. Some days he found it hard to keep still for fifteen whole minutes. His classmates seemed to expect him to create some sort of diversion. But today all he did was read. Lucas got so involved in the story he was reading that he was sorry when the quiet time ended. He decided that he would take the book home for the weekend, instead of leaving it in his desk. He wanted to find out what happened next.

Lucas realized that he was lucky this was Friday. On Thursdays his class had music. How would he have avoided singing with the others? Cricket would have said that singing was talking to music. On Friday, the class had no music, no gym, no art. It was always a long and boring day, but today's challenge made it seem longer than ever.

"I have a treat for you all," said Mrs. Hockaday.

The students looked at her with surprise. "Since Cricket has just gotten a new baby in her family, I stopped by the public library yesterday and borrowed a film about babies. I think you will all find it interesting."

Lucas opened his mouth to ask, "Does it tell us where they come from?" But before he could say a word, he caught Cricket looking triumphant. He had almost lost the bet. He closed his mouth tightly.

Mrs. Hockaday wheeled a projector out of the closet. The film was already set up. She asked Arthur to turn out the lights, and she began to show the film. It was funny to see the little babies eating and slopping food all over. It reminded Lucas of his brothers at home. When the babies' diapers were being changed, there were a few whistles and calls from some of the boys. But Lucas did not make a sound. He wondered if Cricket could see him in the dark. He didn't want her to accuse him of making noises.

The film ended, and it was time to get ready to go home. Mrs. Hockaday walked over to Lucas. "You've been very quiet all day," she said. "Do you feel all right?" She put her hand on his forehead.

Lucas blushed. On any other day he would have made a remark to the teacher, but now he kept silent.

"You may be coming down with something," said Mrs. Hockaday. "Get to bed early tonight and drink a lot of orange juice. I don't want you to get sick and have to miss school."

Lucas was surprised by his teacher's comment. He would have thought she would be glad if he was absent. Maybe she did like him, after all.

"I noticed that he's sick," said Julio. "He's been acting weird all day long."

The bell rang, and Mrs. Hockaday dismissed the class.

"I can't believe you really kept quiet all day," said Cricket as she and Lucas walked out the door.

"You're not going to trick me into talking," said Lucas. "Wait till we get outside."

"I tricked you already!" shouted Cricket. "I fooled you, Lucas Cott. You kept quiet the whole day but you didn't wait until you got out of school. You owe me a dollar bill."

"I do not!" Lucas shouted at her.

"You do so."

"The bell rang. School is over even if we are still

inside it. You said I couldn't keep quiet all day long at school and I did. You owe me a dollar," Lucas said.

"Lucas," said Mrs. Hockaday, coming out into the hallway. "It looks to me like you are making a fine recovery without orange juice. I guess you had a case of too much school. Go home now and enjoy the weekend."

Cricket ran ahead of Lucas and kept running all the way out of the building and into the street. Lucas had a feeling that he wasn't going to get the dollar that he had won. But he also knew that there was no way that Cricket could ever make him pay her a penny.

As he walked home, Lucas thought about all that had happened during the day. He remembered how concerned Mrs. Hockaday had sounded when she thought he was getting sick. He wasn't going to have another bet with Cricket, but maybe he wouldn't call out so much either. He liked it when Mrs. Hockaday liked him. It was a nice feeling.

A Bug
In the Milk

By Johanna Hurwitz

Johanna Hurwitz

Johanna Hurtwitz, age eight

Back when I was in third grade, a boy named Robert sat next to me. Whenever we had art, he used to scoop out some of the thick white paste that we used and eat it. The paste looked like vanilla yogurt but I'm sure it didn't taste like that. Everyone (except our teacher) laughed when Robert ate the paste. He loved being the center of attention and so he continued eating paste all year long. Ugh.

There were other class clowns that I remember from my school days too. Nowadays, I often visit schools all over the country. So far, I have traveled to thirty-six different states. Wherever I have gone, I have seen class clowns. They don't use the same kind of white paste these days, but class clowns keep busy finding other things to do that get a laugh.

Lucas Cott isn't based on any one boy. He is a combination of many of the students I have seen. I laughed while I wrote about him because I thought he was so funny. But at the same time, I was glad that I wasn't Mrs. Hockaday, his teacher. Lucas could be a real pain.

I also enjoyed writing about Cricket Kaufman. She is just the opposite of Lucas. While he is getting in trouble, Cricket is trying hard to be the perfect student. She wants to be the teacher's pet. I wondered to myself if Lucas could behave in class for a whole day. The result was "Lucas Makes a Bet." He tells Cricket that he will not say a single word all day. Instead of calling out, Lucas does not open his mouth to speak at all. Yet there are times in class when one must speak. So Lucas has to be clever and think of ways to keep from speaking. Otherwise he will lose the bet he has made with Cricket.

I remembered a game I used to play with my friends when I was young. The game was called "There's a Bug in the Milk."

One player was the milkman who came to collect payment for the milk. The second player was the customer who refused to pay the bill because, "There's a bug in the milk." Player number one could say anything at all. But player number two could only repeat the same words over and over: "There's a bug in the milk." The game could last a long, long time. And sometimes, player number one, the milkman, might say, "I'm tired of playing. Let's do something else." When player number two, the customer, said, "Okay," the game was over, and the milkman had won. After all, the customer, thinking the game was no longer being played, had been tricked into saying something other than, "There's a bug in the milk."

In that same way, Cricket Kaufman speaks to Lucas as if their bet is over and tricks him so he will speak and lose. It's my opinion that Lucas won the bet and Cricket owes him a dollar. Who do you think won the bet?

Thinking About It

1 You're Lucas! How does it feel to go all day without talking? Are you glad you made the bet?

2 At the end of the day Cricket and Lucas each think they have won the bet. Who is right? Why do you think so?

3 It's a new day and a new bet between Cricket and Lucas. Tell about it. How does it end?

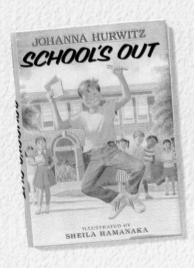

Keeping Track of Lucas Cott

When Lucas Cott sees what summer vacation holds for him, even school begins to look good in *School's Out* by Johanna Hurwitz.

Louella's Song

by Eloise Greenfield
Illustrations by Jan Spivey Gilchrist

Louella leaned forward in her seat and raised her hand. Of all the things in the world she didn't want to do, the thing she most of all *didn't* want to do was sing by herself, on a stage, in front of a lot of people. Everybody knew the song. She didn't know why Miss Simmons had to go and pick her!

She shook her hand in the air. "Miss Simmons," she said. "Miss Simmons, I can't sing by myself."

Miss Simmons looked up from the paper in her hand. "Yes you can, Louella," she said. "I know you've been trying to hide that sweet little voice, but I hear it every time we sing. All you have to do is sing out and make it a sweet big voice."

"But Miss Simmons, . . ." Louella said.

Miss Simmons looked worried. "I've already planned the whole program," she said. "Please, Louella?"

Louella looked around the room for sympathy, but most of her classmates wouldn't look at her. And those who would were frowning. She had to say yes, but she didn't want to. She nodded her head at Miss Simmons, and everybody smiled.

Miss Simmons smiled, too, and looked down at her paper. "Let's see, now," she said. "After Louella's solo, we'll close with 'Lift Every Voice and Sing.' Now, listen, everybody. Tomorrow's the last rehearsal, and when you get here Friday morning, the bus will be here to take us to the hospital. Be sure to . . ."

Louella stopped listening and looked at her classmates again. They would do anything for Miss Simmons. And so would she. Anything *except* sing by herself, on a stage, in front of a lot of people.

It wasn't that she didn't like to sing. At home, she sang a lot, and she sang loud, sang in her big voice—but only in her room with the door closed and just her mirror for an audience. And maybe Dwayne. And when she'd go downstairs, her mother would say, "Why didn't you bring Diana Ross down for some dinner, too?" Or she'd say, "You mean Aretha's up there, too? It must be getting pretty crowded."

But Louella didn't let anybody hear her sing except her brother. And she was going to keep it that way. Dwayne would help her.

"You could tell Mama that you were sick," Dwayne said that night when they were watching television in her room, "and she'd make you stay home."

"Wouldn't nobody believe it," Louella said, "and they'd be all mad and everything. But maybe if I fell down and broke my leg . . ."

"You don't sing with your leg," Dwayne said. "You sing with your . . ." He stopped talking and stared at her.

"What's the matter?" Louella asked.

"You got to hurt your voice!" Dwayne said.

"Fall down and break my *voice?*" Louella said.

"Naw," Dwayne said, laughing. "But something's got to be wrong with your voice."

"I know!" Louella said. "How does this sound?" She made her voice low and scraped it against her throat. "I have a cold. I can't sing."

"Not too good," Dwayne said. "You have to whisper."

Louella practiced whispering and sniffling and sneezing and coughing until it was time to go to bed, and the next day, she sneezed twice at reading time and Miss Simmons handed her a tissue. All through arithmetic, she sniffled loudly. And when she opened her mouth to rehearse her solo, she had a coughing fit and had to run for a drink of water. Miss Simmons told her to rest her voice.

On Friday, when Louella got to school, Miss Simmons was at the door of the bus, crossing names off a list as the children got on.

"Good morning, Miss Simmons," Louella whispered.

Miss Simmons smiled. "Good morning . . . *Louella! Oh, no!*"

Louella nodded her head and tried to look sad.

When they were all on the bus, Miss Simmons announced that Louella had lost her voice and they would all have to sing her song together. Louella kept looking sad, but inside she was smiling. She had fooled them. She didn't have to sing and nobody was mad at her either.

The children at the hospital were waiting for them when they got there. They were sitting in the small auditorium, some of them in the regular seats, some in wheelchairs, and one small boy in a bed.

A girl in a peach-colored dress rolled her wheelchair up to a microphone in front of the stage and welcomed the

class to the hospital. Then Miss Simmons hit the first chord on the piano and they were singing.

Louella whisper-sang and felt good. Soon it would be over. All she had to do was remember for the rest of the day that she couldn't talk.

After the fourth song, the girl in the pretty peach dress took the microphone over to the boy in the bed. She held it to his mouth.

"I made up a thank-you poem," he said, " 'cause I was glad you were coming to sing for us and I want to tell you my poem."

As the boy said his poem, Louella's good feeling started to fade away. By the time he had finished, a very bad feeling had taken its place. She felt too bad to even whisper while they were singing the next song. She just moved her mouth.

She looked at the children in the audience and she looked at her classmates. They were friends, they were all friends, and she was left out. They were giving each other songs and smiles and clapping and even a thank-you poem, but she wasn't giving anything. She wanted to be part of the giving.

She heard Miss Simmons start to play the introduction to her song, and she wanted to sing it. She was scared, but it was something she could give. She stepped out in front of the class the way they had rehearsed at school.

Louella sang softly at first. Then she forgot to be nervous and pushed her voice out into the audience. She *wanted* to give them her music. She liked them, and they liked her.

And then it was time for "Lift Every Voice," and all of her old friends and her new friends were singing together. Some were standing up and those who couldn't stand, lifted their hands in the air.

Louella looked at Miss Simmons. She was smiling as she played. And Louella smiled too.

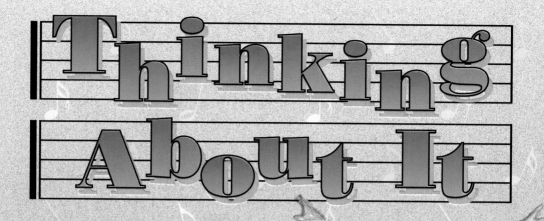

Thinking About It

1 Louella wants to get out of singing her solo. As her best friend, what do you tell her?

2 Ups and downs—Louella's feelings change during the story. What are some of the feelings she has? What causes each of them?

3 You are in the hospital, and you hear Louella sing. What will you tell her after the performance?

Priscilla, Meet Felicity

by Kathleen Leverich

That September morning Priscilla woke up early. "Hurry and dress," said her mother. "You do not want to be late for the first day of school."

Priscilla washed her face. She brushed her teeth. She put on her favorite dress. She put on her socks and her shoes. She opened her drawer, took out her brand-new pencil case, and zipped it open. Inside lay a pink eraser, a blue ballpoint pen, a red marker, and two yellow pencils with sharp points. Priscilla zipped the case shut and carried it downstairs to breakfast.

"Rrrrruf," barked her dog Pow-wow.

"Don't you look nice," said her mother.

"A regular little schoolgirl," said her father.

"Big deal," said her older sister, Eve. "Would somebody please pass the orange juice?"

Priscilla felt a little nervous. "What if none of my friends are in my class?"

"Wrrouu," yipped Pow-wow.

Her mother placed a bowl of cereal in front of Priscilla. She gave her a hug. "Then you will meet new friends."

Priscilla was not so sure.

Priscilla and her mother read the class lists that were posted in the school's front hall.

"There is my name!" Priscilla pointed to the fourth list. "Priscilla Robin."

"Ms. Cobble's class," read Priscilla's mother. "Room 7."

"Is Jill in my class?" asked Priscilla.

"No," said her mother.

"Is Sue in my class?" said Priscilla. "Is Dennis?"

"I am afraid not." Priscilla's mother was looking down the list, too. "Here is a nice name, 'Felicity Doll.' She sounds like a brand-new friend."

Ms. Cobble stood in the doorway to Room 7. "Good morning." She shook hands with Priscilla's mother. "Good morning." She shook hands with Priscilla. "What a lovely new pencil case!"

Ms. Cobble gave Priscilla a big name tag to hang around her neck. "Go right inside," she told Priscilla. "Choose an empty desk and sit down."

Priscilla kissed her mother goodbye. She stepped into the classroom. Lots of boys and girls chattered in the room. Priscilla felt too shy to look at them carefully. She held her pencil case tightly. She looked at the desks.

Most of the desks had a flat top and an opening at one end where you could slide books inside. A few desks looked different. They were big and old. They were made of wood and had slanted tops. The tops opened upward like the top of Priscilla's toy chest. Priscilla watched a boy put his books inside one of those desks. He lifted the desktop high.

"Wow!" thought Priscilla. "I would like one of those desks with the slanty tops." She looked around the classroom. She saw an empty desk near the blackboard. It had a flat top. She saw an empty desk near the coat closet. It had a flat top. She saw an empty desk near the front of the room. It was big and old. It was made of wood and it had a slanty top. Priscilla hurried to the desk. She pulled out a chair and sat down.

"Hey!" said a voice.

Priscilla turned. Beside her stood a curly-haired girl. She wore a ruffly dress. The name on her name tag was too difficult for Priscilla to read.

"You will have to move," said the curly-haired girl. "This desk belongs to me."

Priscilla felt uncertain. Then she felt mad. "This desk was empty when I sat down," she told the curly-haired girl. Priscilla opened the desk. She put her pencil case inside. Beside it she put her lunch box. "This desk is mine."

The curly-haired girl looked at the pencil case. She looked at the lunch box. She smiled a snaky smile at Priscilla. "We could share this desk. Sharing would be the fair thing to do."

"I don't want to share," said Priscilla.

The curly-haired girl poked her in the chest. "Let me share this desk, or I will tell Ms. Cobble you are being selfish."

Priscilla pushed the curly-haired girl's finger away. "All right. But just for now."

"Oh, boy!" said the girl. She dragged up a chair. She jammed it next to Priscilla's. "Move over!" Priscilla had to sit so that one leg was under the desk and one leg was outside it.

At the front of the room Ms. Cobble clapped her hands. "Let's settle down, class."

"Hey," the curly-haired girl nudged Priscilla. She pointed to Priscilla's name tag. "What does that say?"

"Priscilla," she said. She looked at the curly-haired girl's name tag. "What does yours say?"

The curly-haired girl fluffed her curls. "Don't you know how to read?" She pointed to her tag and spelled, "F-e-l-i-c-i-t-y. Felicity Doll."

Ms. Cobble handed out paper. She handed out crayons. She said, "Now, class—"

Felicity raised her hand. "Ms. Cobble!" She waved her hand as hard as she could. "Ms. Cobble!"

"Is something wrong, Felicity?" said Ms. Cobble.

Felicity squirmed in her seat. "I cannot work very well. Priscilla is crowding me."

Ms. Cobble walked over to

where they sat. "What are you two girls doing at the same desk? There are plenty of empty ones. Come, Priscilla. We'll find you a desk of your own."

"But—" said Priscilla.

"Come along," said Ms. Cobble. "We have more things to do this morning than choose desks." She led Priscilla to an ordinary desk with a flat top in the very back row of the classroom. "Now," she said. "Aren't you more comfortable at a desk of your own?"

"Ms. Cobble!" Felicity waved her hand. "Priscilla left this stuff in my desk." She took out Priscilla's lunch box and pencil case and carried them back to Priscilla's new desk.

"Thank you, Felicity," said Ms. Cobble. "I can see that you are going to be an outstanding Class Helper."

Ms. Cobble returned to the front of the room. Felicity returned to her seat.

"Now, class," said Ms. Cobble.

Felicity turned around. "Hey, Priscilla!" she whispered.

"What?"

Felicity stuck out her tongue. She covered her mouth and laughed a silent laugh.

How was your first day of school?" said Priscilla's father that night at dinner.

"Terrible," said Priscilla.

"Rrrrgrrrr." Pow-wow lay under the table at her feet.

"Did you make new friends?" asked her mother.

"I made a new enemy," said Priscilla. "Her name is Felicity Doll. She stole my desk."

"Felicity Doll?" said Eve. "I know Felicity Doll. Felicity Doll is a real snake."

"Eve!" said Priscilla's mother. She was serving the salad. "I am sure Felicity is a lovely girl, once you get to know her."

Eve shook her head. "The one thing worse than having Felicity Doll for an enemy would be having Felicity Doll for a friend."

"I do not need to worry about that," Priscilla said.

The next morning when Priscilla arrived at school she found Felicity waiting beside her desk.

"This is an okay desk," said Felicity. "But my desk is much nicer."

"You stole that desk from me," said Priscilla. She sat down in her chair. She took her pencil case out of her desk. She took out a piece of paper and began to copy the new words Ms. Cobble had written on the blackboard.

Felicity stood beside Priscilla's desk. "Don't be mad, Priscilla. It is not my fault that Ms. Cobble made you move." Felicity leaned on the desk. "I like you, Priscilla."

Priscilla looked up from her paper. She could not believe her ears.

Felicity grabbed Priscilla's hand and squeezed it. "Be my friend. You can sleep over at my house. You can sit next to me at my birthday party . . ." Felicity smiled her snaky smile.

"I have never slept over at a friend's house," said Priscilla. "My sister Eve goes on sleep-overs all the time."

"I have canopy beds," coaxed Felicity. "I have a color TV in my room . . ."

Priscilla freed her hand from Felicity's. "Canopy beds?" Perhaps Felicity was not so bad. "Very well," she said. "I will be your friend."

"Oh, boy!" said Felicity. "Now we can swap pencil cases." She grabbed Priscilla's brand-new pencil case. She pulled her own case from her pocket and dropped it on the desk.

Felicity's case was a mess. The zipper was broken. Inside were two stubby pencils with chew marks. Nothing else.

"I do not want to swap," said Priscilla.

"Just for today." Felicity smiled her snaky smile. "Friends share."

Brnnnnggg! The bell rang.

"So long, pal." Felicity took Priscilla's pencil case and hurried to her desk.

"Felicity!" Priscilla started after her.

"Priscilla, school has begun!" clapped Ms. Cobble. "No more visiting with Felicity. Sit down."

Priscilla sat.

"Now, class," said Ms. Cobble.

Felicity turned around at her desk. "Hey, Priscilla," she hissed. She waved Priscilla's pencil case and snickered.

H ow was your second day of school?" asked Priscilla's father that night at dinner.

"Terrible!" said Priscilla.

"Rrrrgrr," barked Pow-wow from under the dinner table.

"Did you make new friends?" asked Priscilla's mother.

Priscilla stuck her fork prongs into the tablecloth. "Felicity Doll wants to be my friend."

"That's nice," said Priscilla's mother. She passed Priscilla a plate of beef stew. "I am glad you two girls made up."

"Pris-cil-la," said Eve. "May I see you for a moment in the kitchen?"

Priscilla followed Eve through the swinging door.

Pow-wow followed Priscilla.

Eve shook her head. "You've been at school two days, Priscilla, and you've already made a giant mistake."

"Making friends with Felicity?" guessed Priscilla.

"Felicity does not know how to be a friend," said Eve. "Felicity knows how to be a snake."

"Rrrrgrr," barked Pow-wow.

Priscilla nodded. "Yesterday Felicity stole my desk. Today she took my pencil case."

"You need someone to stick up for you," said Eve. "Do you want me to make Felicity give your things back?"

Priscilla wanted her things back. "But," she thought, "Felicity will trap me again with another one of her tricks. . ."

"Eve?" called their mother from the dining room. "Priscilla? Dinner is getting cold!"

"Thank you," Priscilla told Eve. "But I think I'd better stick up for myself."

The next morning Felicity wanted to trade lunch boxes. "I have a lunch box," said Priscilla. "You carry your lunch in a paper bag."

"Friends share." Felicity smiled her snaky smile.

Before Priscilla knew what happened, Felicity carried off Priscilla's lunch box. Felicity put the lunch box inside the beautiful desk that should have been Priscilla's. She put it right next to the brand-new pencil case that Priscilla could only see from a distance.

At lunch Felicity spilled tomato juice on her pink sweater.

"Friends share," Felicity told Priscilla. Before Priscilla knew it, Felicity had taken Priscilla's soft yellow sweater.

"What will I do with this?" Priscilla wrinkled her nose. Felicity had left her the soggy pink mess.

Felicity Doll has gone too far!" Eve said to Priscilla after dinner that night. "She took your pencil case, and your lunch box, and now your sweater—"

"Don't forget my desk," said Priscilla.

"She cannot push around my little sister!" Eve made a fist. "Tomorrow—"

"Eve," said Priscilla, "let me try one last time."

The next morning Priscilla arrived at school. Felicity waited beside her desk.

"I did not do my homework," said Felicity. "Lend me your paper. I will copy the answers."

Priscilla opened her mouth to say "NO!"

"Well?" said Felicity.

Priscilla shut her mouth. She had an idea. "Here is my homework." She handed Felicity her paper. She smiled a Felicity smile.

"Friends share," she said.

Felicity looked at the paper. She looked hard at Priscilla. "Is there something wrong with this homework—?"

Brnnnnggg! The bell rang.

"Settle down, class." Ms. Cobble clapped her hands.

Felicity snatched Priscilla's paper and hurried to her seat.

Priscilla watched Felicity take off *her* soft yellow sweater. She watched Felicity hang it over the back of *her* chair. She watched Felicity take a brand-new pencil out of *her* pencil case. Felicity began to copy *her* homework— "Ms. Cobble!" Priscilla raised her hand. She waved it.

Ms. Cobble turned from the blackboard. "Priscilla, whatever is the trouble?"

Priscilla took a deep breath. "Felicity Doll is sitting at my desk."

Ms. Cobble looked at Felicity. She looked at Priscilla. "We already settled this matter, Priscilla."

"Ask Felicity whose lunch box is in that desk," said Priscilla.

"Felicity?" said Ms. Cobble.

"Wel-l-l-l," said Felicity.

"Ask her whose pencil case is in that desk," said Priscilla.

Ms. Cobble looked stern.

"Uhnnn—" said Felicity.

"That is my yellow sweater hanging over the back of Felicity's chair," said Priscilla.

Ms. Cobble frowned.

Felicity looked at her feet.

"That is my homework on top of the desk," said Priscilla.

"Fe-li-city!" said Ms. Cobble. "Is this true?"

Felicity's voice sounded squeaky. "Yes."

"Priscilla," said Ms. Cobble, "Felicity, I think you had better change desks."

"I'll get you," hissed Felicity as she passed Priscilla.

Priscilla sat down at the beautiful desk. "I doubt it," she thought.

How was school today?" asked Priscilla's father that night at dinner.

"Rrrruf," yipped Pow-wow.

"Excellent," said Priscilla.

Priscilla's mother asked, "Did you play with your friend Felicity Doll?"

"Felicity Doll is no longer my friend," said Priscilla. "Please pass the Brussels sprouts."

"Not your friend?" Priscilla's mother looked concerned. "Whatever happened?"

Eve choked on her macaroni. "Yes, Priscilla, tell us what happened."

Pow-wow yawned. **"Eeeehh."**

Priscilla took a sip of milk. She smoothed the sleeves of her soft yellow sweater. "After school today, Felicity stopped me. She told me that we are no longer friends. 'We are enemies!' she said."

Priscilla's mother sighed.

Priscilla's father shook his head.

"Felicity has a new best friend," said Priscilla. "Her name is Lucille Bingay."

"How sad!" said Eve, but she was giggling. "You must feel just awful."

Priscilla speared a Brussels sprout. "I don't feel nearly as awful as poor Lucille."

Thinking About It

1 Felicity Doll is the new girl at school and she's sitting right next to you! Don't forget. You should be friendly to new students. What do you plan to do?

2 Priscilla's mom tells her Felicity can be a friend. Priscilla's sister calls Felicity a "snake." What do you think? Why?

3 Maybe Felicity isn't all bad. What advice would you give to Priscilla about being friends with Felicity?

Priscilla and Felicity Return!

Will Felicity ever change? Can enemies ever be friends? Find out in *Best Enemies, Again* by Kathleen Leverich.

TACKY
the Penguin

by Helen Lester

Illustrations by Lynn Munsinger

There once lived a penguin.
His home was a nice icy land he shared
with his companions.

His companions were named
Goodly, Lovely, Angel, Neatly, and Perfect.

His name was Tacky.
Tacky was an odd bird.

Every day Goodly, Lovely, Angel, Neatly, and Perfect greeted each other quietly and politely.

Tacky greeted them with a hearty slap on the back and a loud "What's happening?"

Goodly, Lovely, Angel, Neatly, and Perfect always marched

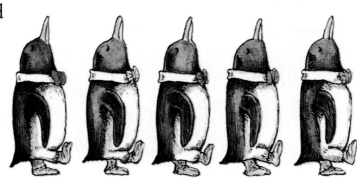

1-2-3-4, 1-2-3-4.

Tacky always marched 1-2-3,

4-2,

3-6-0,

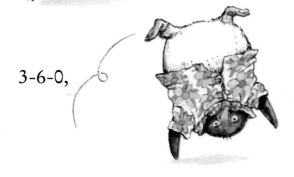

2½,

0.

His companions were graceful divers.
Tacky liked to do splashy cannonballs.

Goodly, Lovely, Angel, Neatly, and Perfect always sang pretty songs like "Sunrise on the Iceberg."

Tacky always sang songs like "How Many Toes Does a Fish Have?"

Tacky was an odd bird.

One day the penguins heard the *thump . . . thump . . . thump* of feet in the distance. This could mean only one thing. Hunters had come.

They came with maps and traps and rocks and locks,
and they were rough and tough.
As the *thump . . . thump . . . thump*
drew closer, the penguins could hear
the growly voices chanting,

"We're gonna catch some pretty penguins,
And we'll march 'em with a switch,
And we'll sell 'em for a dollar,
And get rich, rich, RICH!"

Goodly, Lovely, Angel, Neatly, and Perfect ran away in fright. They hid behind a block of ice.

Tacky stood alone. The hunters marched right up to him, chanting,

"We're gonna catch some pretty penguins,
And we'll march 'em with a switch,
And we'll sell 'em for a dollar,
And get rich, rich, RICH!"

"What's happening?" blared Tacky, giving one hunter an especially hearty slap on the back. They growled, "We're hunting for penguins. That's what's happening."

"PENNNNGUINS?" said Tacky. "Do you mean those birds that march neatly in a row?"
And he marched,

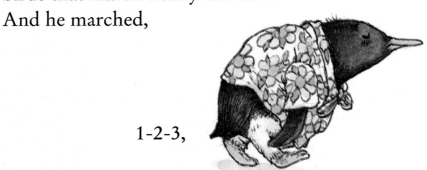

1-2-3,

4-2,

3-6-0,

2½,

0.

The hunters looked puzzled.

"Do you mean those birds that dive so gracefully?"
Tacky asked.

And he did a splashy cannonball.
The hunters looked wet.

"Do you mean those birds that sing such pretty songs?"
Tacky began to sing, and from behind the block of ice
came the voices of his companions, all singing as loudly
and dreadfully as they could.

"HOW MANY TOES DOES A FISH HAVE?

AND HOW MANY WINGS ON A COW?

I WONDER. YUP,

I WONDER."

The hunters could not stand the horrible singing.
This could not be the land of the pretty penguins.
They ran away with their hands clasped tightly

over their ears, leaving behind their maps and traps
and rocks and locks, and not looking at all rough
and tough.

Goodly, Lovely, Angel, Neatly, and Perfect hugged
Tacky.

Tacky was an odd bird but a very nice bird
to have around.

THINKING
About It

1 Do you know anyone who sometimes does things like Tacky? Are you ever a Tacky? Is it useful to be a Tacky? Tell about it.

2 There are rhymes and jingles in the story. What makes them funny? How could you make them come alive?

3 Oh, no! Something else is coming to the nice icy land. Who or what is it? How will Tacky and his friends get by? What will they do?

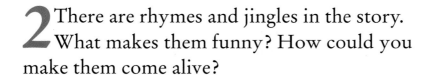

Tacky's Back

Tacky and his friends enter the Penguin Cheering Contest. Will Tacky be able to get the cheering routine right when they go before the judges? Find out in *Three Cheers for Tacky* by Helen Lester.

O·L·D
H·E·N·R·Y

BY JOAN W. BLOS

ILLUSTRATIONS BY STEPHEN GAMMELL

The story begins when a stranger appears

and moves into a house that was vacant for years.

No one thought he meant to stay;

the house was drafty, dark and gray,

and more than seven years had passed

since anyone had lived there last.

HOUSE
FOR
RENT

He meant to stay.

He had no doubt.

It suited him from inside out,

and in its vast and dusty spaces

all the things he had

found places.

That Henry!

The neighbors watched him moving in

and promised each other he'd soon begin

to fix things up a bit.

He did not think of it.

With money enough to pay the rent,

his books, birds, and cooking pots,

he was content

and never did notice (or else didn't care)

that people whispered everywhere:

"That place

is a disgrace."

"At least," they remarked,

"you would think that he could

show a little respect for the neighborhood."

"That place is a disgrace."

At last they decided to form a committee

and went to him saying, "We are proud of our city.

If you'd only help out, think how good it would look—"

"Excuse me." He bowed,

and went back to his book.

That Henry.

Then they fined him fines. They threatened jail.

They wrote him long letters and sent them by mail:

"Dear Henry . . ."

Still the hollyhocks wilted, unwatered, unkept;

the gatepost stayed crooked, the walk stayed unswept.

And things went on as they'd begun,

and he angered his neighbors, one by one.

"So unfriendly!"

"Never talks!"

"Can't we *make* him sweep his walks?"

"No, there's nothing we can do—

You nasty Polly! Shoo, bird, shoo!"

On a day in November they sought the advice

of the mayor, who suggested being nice.

"Being *nice?*"

"Please,

try it twice."

But when two of the ladies baked him a pie,

he said, "I'm not hungry. No, thank you. Good-bye."

And when three of the men said they'd shovel his snow,

he quickly said: "No!"

"We told you so!"

Now Henry, too, had had his fill.

That night he grumbled, "I never *will*

live like the rest of them, neat and the same.

I am sorry I came."

Then he packed some things in shopping bags
and tied the rest in three old rags.

He didn't make plans, he just left a short note, a
hastily written: G o n e t o D a k o t a

He taped it to the big front door.

And no one lived there

anymore.

His day lilies bloomed; his phlox grew tall.

They picked his apples in the fall.

They picked his apples and now and then

someone would ask, "Remember when . . . ?

Remember when . . . ?

Remember when . . ."

Later still, in winter's snow,

they asked one another, "Where did he go?"

"Will he come again?"

"His house looks so empty, so dark in the night."

"And having him gone doesn't make us more right."

That Henry.

"Maybe, some other time, we'd get along

not thinking that somebody *has* to be wrong."

"And we don't have to make such a terrible fuss

because everyone isn't exactly like us."

Meanwhile, Old Henry, to his great surprise,

was missing the neighbors who'd brought him the pies.

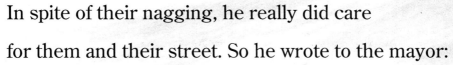

In spite of their nagging, he really did care

for them and their street. So he wrote to the mayor:

Dear Mr. Mayor,

I am finding it hard
to be far from my house
and my tree and my yard.

If I mended the gate,
and I shoveled the snow,
would they not scold my birds?
Could I let my grass grow?

Please write and tell me
the answers so then we
can all get together.

Sincerely yours,

Henry

T·H·I·N·K·I·N·G
ABOUT IT

1. Old Henry has just moved into your
neighborhood, and the neighbors want him
to clean up his house and yard. It's his house.
It's his yard. Should he have to do it?

2. It's a poem! It's a story! It's *Old Henry!*
What do you think? Is it a poem, a story,
or maybe both? Why?

3. As the mayor, what do you think of Old
Henry's letter? What will you write back
to him?

CHANG'S PAPER PONY

By Eleanor Coerr
Illustrations by Byron Gin

#

Chang and Grandpa Li were peeling potatoes in the kitchen of the Gold Ditch Hotel. Suddenly Chang stopped.

"I hear horses!" he cried, and ran to the door.

"If only I had a pony," he told Grandpa Li, "I would never be lonely."

"Next year," said Grandpa Li, "the miners will bring their families. You will not be lonely then."

But Chang was not sure. He remembered the day he and Grandpa Li had arrived in San Francisco. He remembered how some boys had thrown stones at them.

"American children hate us," Chang said.

Grandpa Li shook his head. "They do not hate us," he said. "They just do not understand us."

"I would rather have a pony. Then I would really have a *pengyo*—a friend," Chang said.

Grandpa Li smiled. "You have friends now," he said. "There is your teacher, and the barber, and the blacksmith. And don't forget Big Pete."

"They are too old to play with," Chang said. "But I could play with a pony."

Grandpa Li pointed to a painting tacked above the stove. "That is the only pony we can afford," he said. "Now finish peeling the potatoes. Hungry miners will soon come for my good supper."

Chang did as he was told. He also set the tables, brought water from the well, and carried in wood for the stove. All the time he wished he had a pony.

TROUBLE

Some miners were rough. They liked to yank Chang's pigtail. Chang tried to keep his pigtail out of their reach. And he was always polite. When a miner asked him his name, Chang bowed low and said, "My humble name is Chang."

The miner slapped his knee. "Doesn't that pop your eyeballs!" he cried. Everyone laughed.

Chang ran into the kitchen. "I want to go home to China," he said.

Grandpa Li held him close. "You know we can't go back," he said. "There is a war in China."

"But those miners—why are they so mean?" asked Chang.

Grandpa Li sighed. "They left their hearts at home," he said. "All they can think about is gold. And gold fever makes them a little crazy."

After supper Chang took a bath in the big tub. Then he tightened his pigtail and put on clean clothes. He walked down the dusty main street to his lessons. Chang stopped to look at the horses in the town stable. "When I have a pony," he thought, "I will keep him here."

Scholar See Yow taught Chang to read and write English. How Chang hated it! The words looked like ugly worms wiggling across the paper.

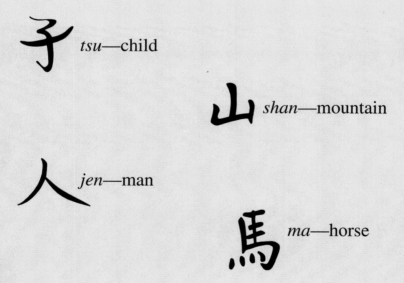

子 *tsu*—child

山 *shan*—mountain

人 *jen*—man

馬 *ma*—horse

Chang liked painting Chinese words with a pointed brush and black ink. Each word looked like a picture: *tsu*—child, *jen*—man, *shan*—mountain. When he came to *ma*—horse, Chang began to daydream.

CRAAAAACK! Scholar See Yow's stick came down across Chang's skinny back.

"If you don't stop playing," the teacher said, "you will be an empty bamboo—good for nothing."

Chang swallowed hard. He did not care about being an empty bamboo. All he wanted was a pony.

That night Chang hugged his pillow. He pretended it was his pony's neck. He could almost feel its soft nose and hear it breathing.

BIG PETE

Things got better for Chang when Big Pete came to Gold Ditch. Big Pete was the tallest, strongest man Chang had ever seen. He never pulled Chang's pigtail or teased him.

It was getting very busy in Gold Ditch. More and more miners came every day. They dug for gold in the mountains. They panned for gold in the rivers. They weighed their gold nuggets on Big Pete's scales. Tiny flakes of gold fell to the floor. The men only cared about big nuggets of gold.

One day Big Pete showed Chang some of the big nuggets. That was when Chang got an idea.

"Big Pete, will you show me how to look for gold?" he asked. "I need gold to buy a pony."

Big Pete looked at Chang. "A pony costs a heap of money," he said.

"Please," said Chang. "I will clean your cabin and scrub your floor."

Big Pete laughed. "Tell you what," he said. "If your grandpa says okay, I will take you tomorrow."

Chang gave a shout and ran to the Gold Ditch Hotel.

"Please, please let me go," he begged.

"Ahummmmmm," said Grandpa Li. Chang held his breath and waited. Finally, Grandpa nodded. "Just this once," he said. "Maybe the fat God of Luck will smile upon you."

GOLD FEVER

Early the next morning Grandpa Li packed a lunch for Chang and Big Pete. Chang took a bag to put the gold in. Big Pete lifted him onto his horse. "HY-AAAAAH!" he yelled, and they rode off.

At a deep ditch Big Pete handed Chang a shovel and pail. The ground was like rock. Big Pete loosened it with a pick. Chang scooped up the earth with his shovel.

Big Pete showed Chang how to pan for gold in the river. He poured some earth into a pan. Then he rocked and twisted it in the water. When the mud washed away, there were sand and pebbles. But not a speck of gold.

Chang worked hard. The sun grew hot. Sweat ran down his face, and his hands got blistered.

"Go easy, pardner," said Big Pete. "The gold will not run away."

But Chang could not slow down. He wanted his pony! Suddenly, Chang let out a shout. "YOWEEE! GOLD!"

Flakes of gold glittered among the pebbles and sand in his pan. Chang carefully poured it all into his bag. He and Big Pete galloped into Gold Ditch. "Now I can have my pony!" Chang shouted.

Chang spread the treasure on the kitchen table. Big Pete helped him blow away all the sand and dirt. Chang stared at what was left.

"That will not even buy a goat," he said sadly. "Now I will never have a pony."

THE REAL PONY

In the morning Chang kept his promise. He took a broom to Big Pete's cabin and began to sweep. Suddenly he saw something glittering between the wooden boards. Chang knelt down for a closer look. "Gold!" he whispered.

The pieces were no bigger than a pinhead, but there were lots of them. Maybe enough to buy a pony! He put all the gold flakes into a pail and ran home to show Grandpa Li.

"Now I can buy a pony, for sure!" Chang cried.

Grandpa Li gave Chang a long, hard look. "Of course you will give the gold to Big Pete," he said. "It was in his cabin."

"I . . . I guess so," said Chang. His dream of having a pony faded away.

"By jingo!" Big Pete said. "I never knew there was so much gold in my floor."

Big Pete took the gold to the bank in Sacramento. Chang took down the paper pony and tried to forget his dream.

One afternoon Chang heard a clippity-clop.

"That's Big Pete's horse," said Grandpa Li.

"I know," said Chang. Slowly, he walked to the door. There was Big Pete. He was leading a handsome pony.

"He is all yours, pardner," Big Pete said. "I bought him with your share of the gold."

Chang gently reached out and rubbed the pony's moist nose. The pony nuzzled Chang's fingers and whinnied softly. A big smile spread across Chang's face. "I think he likes me," he said.

Big Pete swung Chang up onto the pony's back. Chang felt he would burst for joy.

"My own pony!" he cried. "I will call you Pengyo." Chang leaned over and whispered into the pony's ear, "I love you, Pengyo." Pengyo gave a little snort, as if he understood.

California mining camp, 1852

SEARCHING FOR GOLD

By Eleanor Coerr

n the middle of the last century, around the year 1848, a man in California found a dull, yellowish rock the size of his thumb.

GOLD! When news of his discovery spread, people rushed to California to get more rocks like it. Carrying picks and shovels, they hurried as fast as they could—by ship, stagecoach, horse, and on foot.

Stories grew taller and taller and further from the truth. When the people over in China heard that the streets of San Francisco were paved with gold, they came too—by the thousands. Then they packed onto steamboats that sat on the Sacramento River like fat ducks with big tails. Up the river they chugged toward the mines.

◀ *San Francisco during the California Gold Rush*

When I read about the Chinese in California gold mines and the terrible way some of them were treated, I decided to write a story. The facts about cruelty toward the Chinese in those days are buried. I had to dig them out. That was the fun part. It is called research.

I visited a historical library and read all the old books I could find about the lives of the Chinese miners. Every now and then I came across facts that shone like gems—facts about the Chinese culture and family life as well as mining. My imagination wove them together into *Chang's Paper Pony.*

I hope that you enjoyed the story and understand in a small way that part of our past. You might even read historical books and discover facts that shine like gems about the Chinese who came to America and the way they helped our country become great.

Eleanor Coerr

THINKING ABOUT IT

 Chang wishes he had a pony. What do you wish you could do or have? What can you do to try to get your wish?

 Chang jumps in a time machine and comes to your house. What can you show him that they didn't have back in the days of the California Gold Rush? What will interest him most?

 Now that Chang has his pony, what will happen next?

THE GREAT FLAMINGO ROUNDUP

from *Ranger Rick Magazine*
by Claire Miller
Photographs by C. C. Lockwood

Wall-to-wall flamingos crowd the shore of a lagoon in Mexico. Find out why these birds might be in trouble, and what two kids did to help them.

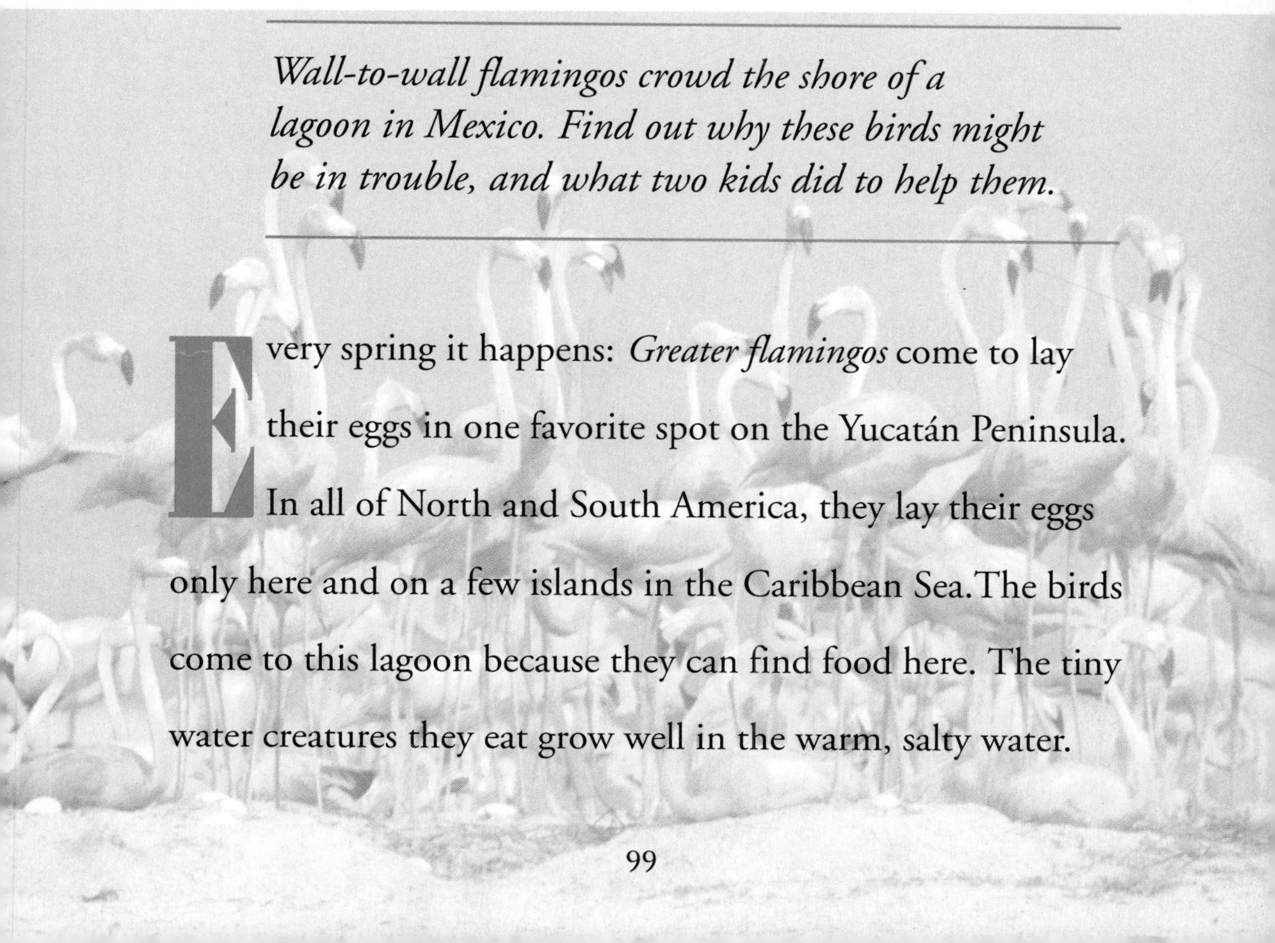

Every spring it happens: *Greater flamingos* come to lay their eggs in one favorite spot on the Yucatán Peninsula. In all of North and South America, they lay their eggs only here and on a few islands in the Caribbean Sea. The birds come to this lagoon because they can find food here. The tiny water creatures they eat grow well in the warm, salty water.

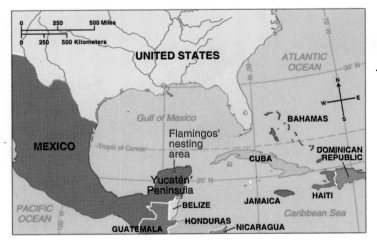

The dot shows where the flamingos nest on the Yucatán Peninsula.

Now scientists are worried that this flock may face trouble. A company that sells salt is planning to change the lagoon so that most of the salt will settle in one part of the lagoon. Then the company will be able to collect the salt more easily. But if the saltiness of the water changes, the tiny water creatures may die. Then the birds will not be able to find food, so they won't use the lagoon as a nesting spot anymore.

But no one knows for sure what might happen if the amount of salt in the water changes. That's why two scientists, Alexander Sprunt from the United States and Jorge Correa from Mexico, teamed up. They wanted to learn all they could about the birds and the lagoon. The first thing they wanted to do was to catch some young birds and put bands on their legs. The bands would help the scientists keep track of where the birds go. But they

100

needed help with catching the birds, and that's where the kids came in.

Karina Boege lives about a four-hour drive from the lagoon. She got a phone call from Dr. Correa. He asked if she would like to help catch flamingos for the study. "I told him yes," says Karina, "but then I began to worry. Were those tall pink birds with big beaks something I actually wanted to *catch?* I could hardly sleep the night before we went, I was so excited—and worried!"

But it was different for Jason Kennedy, who was visiting Mexico from his home in Vermont. When he agreed to help, he found out right away that they'd be catching flamingo *chicks.*

Karina and Jason catch the birds and hand them out to runners.

THE BIG CHASE

"My dad and I crossed the lagoon by boat," Jason explains. "The flamingos were standing in shallow water near an island. And on the island Mr. Sprunt was telling people what to do. They were setting up cages and getting other things ready. I was glad when he picked me to go out into the shallow water and round up the young flamingos."

When Karina arrived on the island, Mr. Sprunt picked her to run after the birds too. She was bursting with excitement when she started toward the birds. "The adult flamingos all twisted their long necks so they could stare at us," she reports. "Suddenly they raised their wings and took off. What a sight—they looked like a pink cloud in the sky! Then I noticed their gray chicks had been left behind in the shallow water. They were too young to fly. Finally I realized that we'd be catching just the *chicks!*"

As soon as the adult flamingos flew off, the frightened chicks started to dash in all directions. Jason and Karina had to move fast to shoo them into the cages. Other people helped too, and soon both cages were full.

Jason went into one cage and Karina into the other. Next their job was to catch each bird and hand it out to a runner. The runners quickly took the birds to the scientists. "When I caught my first flamingo," Karina remembers, "I held the bird in my hands for a minute, and I could feel its heart thumping. I had this marvelous feeling that I was helping nature."

Karina is one of many helpers to put bands on 500 birds.

HERE COME THE BANDS

Soon the kids were catching the chicks so fast that others could hardly keep up. As quickly as they could, the scientists put a band on each leg of each chick.

"The first band we put on was blue," Mr. Sprunt explains. "That tells us what year they were banded. Each year that we study the birds, we'll give them a different colored band. Then in years to come, we can just look at a colored band on a bird's leg, and we'll know its age."

And what was the second band for? "Well, I like to think of the other band as a name tag," Mr. Sprunt continues. "Each bird is given its own numbered band so we can tell it from all other birds. We write down the numbers and where the birds were banded. When people in other areas catch those birds, they tell us. Then we can work to protect those areas too. We're just beginning to learn all the things we need to know in order to help the birds."

And what do the kids think about all this? "I hope I can go to Mexico again and help band flamingos," Jason says.

"I would like to help again too," Karina agrees. "And next time maybe I'll see some adult flamingos with blue bands. They might be the very same birds I held when they were just gray chicks!"

Thinking About It

1 Does a flamingo roundup sound like something you would like to try? Would you help Jason and Karina? Tell about it.

2 If flamingos could understand you, how would you explain to them what the scientists are doing?

3 What kinds of wildlife do you have in your neighborhood? What can you do to help them?

More Animals in Trouble

Bats, tigers, and more animals fighting to survive come to life with pop-up illustrations in *Animals in Danger* by William McCay.

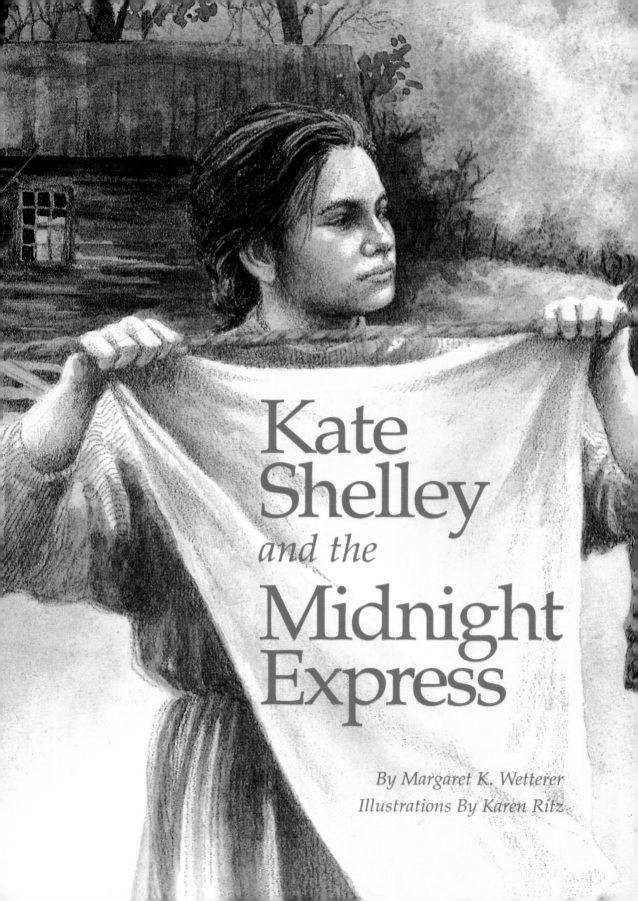

Kate
Shelley
and the
Midnight
Express

By Margaret K. Wetterer
Illustrations By Karen Ritz

Moingona, Iowa
July 6, 1881

Fifteen-year-old Kate Shelley pulled the sheets from the line. A terrible storm was coming. Kate could feel it in the air. A cold wind rose as she carried the heavy basket back to the house. Black clouds rolled in. The sky grew dark.

Kate stood at the kitchen window with her younger sisters and brother. They saw lightning flash. They heard thunder crack in the hills. Then the rain came.

As the rain
poured down, they watched
the water rising in Honey Creek.
Soon it overflowed its banks
and flooded part of the yard.

"I'm going to let the animals
out of the barn," Kate said. "If the
water keeps rising, they could drown."

"Be careful you don't slip in the
water," her mother warned.

Kate ran down the hill. She waded through
muddy water to the barn. She led out the two horses
and shooed them off to higher ground. She drove the cows
up the hill. Then she hurried back to the barn. She picked
up some piglets and carried them to the house. By this
time, she was soaked to the skin.

Kate put on dry clothes and went back to the window.
The rain had not let up. The floodwater was coming closer
to the house.

When lightning flashed, Kate could see the shining
railroad tracks. They ran along the other side of Honey
Creek. Kate peered through the rain, trying to see the

railroad bridge over Honey Creek. How was it holding up in this storm?

After supper, the younger children went to bed. Nine-year-old Mayme wanted to stay awake with her mother and Kate. They sat at the kitchen table, talking about the dangers of the storm. They were worried about the men out working on the railroad.

At midnight, an express train would pass the Moingona station without stopping. It would cross the long bridge over the Des Moines River. Then it would cross the bridge over Honey Creek, near Kate's house. Were the bridges safe?

Shortly after eleven o'clock, Kate and her mother heard an engine chugging slowly down the tracks. Railroad men were checking the tracks and bridges before the express came through. They were heading toward the bridge over Honey Creek.

Suddenly, the engine's bell rang wildly. Then Kate heard a terrible crack. She knew at once that the bridge had broken. Kate heard the hot engine hiss as it hit the cold water. She jumped to her feet.

"Oh, Mother," she cried. "They've gone down in Honey Creek. I must go help."

The crash woke the children. They watched silently as Kate pulled on a jacket and an old straw hat. Then she lit her father's railroad lantern.

"You can't go, Kate," her mother said. "It's too dangerous."

"I have to go, Mother," Kate answered. "Someone may still be alive in Honey Creek. And I have to stop the midnight express."

"Please, Kate," her mother cried. "Don't go. The floodwaters are almost at our door."

"If that were Father down there, wouldn't we want someone to help him?" asked Kate.

"You're right," her mother agreed. "Go ahead then, but be careful! We'll be praying for you."

Kate could not cross the flooded yard to get to the broken bridge. Instead, she started up a path behind her house. She would reach the tracks where they ran through the hills. Water poured down the hillside. Kate climbed over fallen trees. Her skirt caught in wet brambles. Her

shoes sank in mud. But she held her father's lantern before her and kept going. At last she reached the tracks.

Kate ran along the tracks back to the broken bridge. She looked out over the dark waters of Honey Creek. She could not see the engine or any of the crew. Had they all drowned? Then Kate thought she heard a shout. In the roar of the storm, she was not sure. She listened again. Yes. Someone was calling.

Lightning flashed. Kate saw someone holding on to the branches of a treetop just above the water. Thunder boomed. As it faded, Kate heard voices calling again. She could hear two men's voices now, but she couldn't make out their words above the howl of the storm.

"Hang on! Hang on!" Kate shouted. "I'll get help." Kate swung the lantern back and forth. Now the men would know she had heard them and was going for help.

Kate began to run toward the Moingona station. There wasn't much time. She had to get to the station before midnight, before the express. Kate ran along the tracks. Even before she reached the Des Moines River bridge, she could hear the rush of the floodwater. She held up the lantern to light her way over the bridge. But as she did, a fierce wind blew out the lantern's small flame.

Kate stared into the darkness. To reach the Moingona station, she had to cross this river. The long wooden bridge stretched before her. Beside the tracks was a narrow walkway. Some of its boards were missing. There was no handrail to hold. Kate was afraid to cross this bridge even in daylight. Could she do it now, in this storm, in the dark?

Kate thought of the men in Honey Creek. She thought of all the people on the train speeding toward the broken bridge. She got down on her hands and knees and began to crawl across. Kate felt for gaps in the walkway so she

would not fall through. Nails and splinters cut her hands and knees and tore her skirt. She gripped the steel rail of the tracks to keep the wind from sweeping her over the side.

Trees and logs in the flooded river crashed against the bridge, making it shake. When she reached the middle of the bridge, great flashes of lightning suddenly lit the night. She looked up. A huge tree was coming down the river straight toward her. Surely it would crash through the bridge. Kate closed her eyes and prayed.

In the next moment, the river pulled the tree down under the water. Kate felt the tree scrape beneath the walkway. Then it was gone.

Kate was shaking with fear, but she could not stop to rest. She knew it must be almost midnight. She had to reach the station before the midnight express.

At last, Kate's hand touched land. She had crossed the river. The Moingona station was less than a half mile ahead. She got to her feet and began to run. Her heart pounded. Her throat ached. But through the rain, she saw the lights of the station.

Kate threw open the station house door. The men inside turned and stared. Kate's clothes were torn and muddy. Water dripped from her old straw hat. She tried to speak, but no words came.

At last she gasped, "The engine went down in Honey Creek. Stop the express." Then she sagged to the floor.

"The girl must be crazy," someone said.

But the station agent knew Kate. "She means a bridge is out," he shouted. "We must stop the express."

He rushed to the telegraph and tapped out a message to Ogden, the station before Moingona. STOP EXPRESS . . . BRIDGE OUT . . . STOP EXPRESS.

Another man grabbed a lantern. Then he ran out to the platform. He would flag down the express if the telegraph message was too late. The express, with two hundred people aboard, was still speeding toward the broken bridge.

But Kate's warning had come in time. Railroad men stopped the train at Ogden. It was the last telegraph message sent or received that night. The storm knocked out telegraph service for forty miles along the line. Someone helped Kate to a chair. Someone gave her a glass of water. "Two men are still alive in Honey Creek," Kate said. "I saw them holding on to trees in the water."

"Let's try to save them before they're washed away," a man said.

"Would you help us, Kate?" another man asked. "Would you show us where they are?"

Kate rode the engine with the rescue party. They crossed the Des Moines River on the same bridge Kate had crawled over. The engine stopped at the broken bridge on Honey Creek.

Everyone shouted, and the men in the water answered. They were still hanging on. But there was no way to reach them from that side of the flooded creek.

Kate led the rescue party into the hills behind her house. She led them through the woods to a bridge farther upstream. There, they crossed Honey Creek and at last rescued the two exhausted men.

Kate went home and slept for a long time. When she awoke, her family, friends, and neighbors greeted her happily. They wanted to hear about her adventure. Reporters came. Newspapers across the country told the story of her bravery. Soon the whole nation knew about Kate Shelley. The railroad company gave Kate one hundred dollars and a lifetime pass on the railroad. Poems and songs were written in her honor. The State of Iowa awarded her a gold medal.

But of all the honors given to her, Kate liked the one from her railroad friends best. Whenever she rode the train home, they stopped it to let her off right in front of her own house.

Pulling the Theme Together

1 What did you see in your mind as you read about Kate Shelley? At first you didn't know Kate very well. But as you read, you got to know her better. What did you think of her? How did you feel when you found out that the story really happened?

2 Be one of the characters from this book. Tell what you learned from what happened to you.

3 You can choose one or more characters from this book to be in a TV series. Who will it be? What will happen in the series? Who will watch it?

Books to Enjoy

Yoshiko Uchida · Joanna Yardley

The Bracelet

by Yoshiko Uchida
Philomel, 1993
Emi and her family are sent to an internment camp for Japanese Americans during World War II. Emi doesn't want to leave her friends, but she learns that she doesn't need a physical reminder of her friendships.

The Kid Next Door and Other Headaches: Stories About Adam Joshua

by Janice Lee Smith
Illustrations by Dick Gackenbach
HarperCollins, 1984
Adam Joshua and his best friend, Nelson, are as different as night and day. However, with a little giving and taking, they manage to stay best friends.

The All New Jonah Twist

by Natalie Honeycutt
Macmillan, 1986
Jonah Twist is determined to be a perfect third-grader, but Granville, a new kid in the neighborhood, makes third grade a real challenge for Jonah.

Seven Kisses in a Row

by Patricia MacLachlan
HarperCollins, 1983
Emma and Zach teach their aunt and uncle a few things about being parents. Along the way, the kids learn a couple of things about being adults.

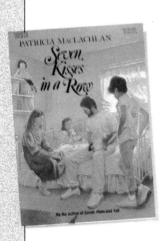

Antarctica

Written and illustrated by Helen Cowcher
Soundprints, 1990
Did you know that the male emperor penguin balances the penguin egg on top of his feet for two months before it hatches? This and more amazing facts about penguins can be found in this book.

Walking the Road to Freedom: A Story About Sojourner Truth

by Jeri Ferris
Carolrhoda, 1988
Sojourner Truth devoted her life to helping other people. Walking from town to town, she spoke out against slavery and in favor of women's rights.

Literary Terms

Mood

Mood is the feeling you get when you read a story. The author lets you know by what the characters say that the mood of *Kate Shelley and the Midnight Express* is serious and suspenseful. When Kate wants to go into the storm, her mother says it is too dangerous. How do the pictures help make the mood of the story serious?

Narrative Poem

Old Henry has rhyme and it tells a story. This is called a **narrative poem.** In the poem, you get to know Henry. You learn about his life in his new neighborhood.

Plot

The **plot** is often interesting because a character has a problem to solve. Kate Shelley's problem is how to stop the express train during the storm. To solve her problem, Kate has to win a fight against nature (the storm). In "Priscilla, Meet Felicity," Priscilla's problem is another person, Felicity. Louella's problem is her fear of singing alone.

Realistic Fiction

Realistic fiction is a story that could really happen. The characters are like real people. Do Lucas Cott and Cricket Kaufman act like some of your friends? The things that happen between Priscilla and Felicity also seem like things that could happen in most schools. "Priscilla, Meet Felicity" and "Lucas Makes a Bet" are both realistic fiction.

Setting

The **setting** is when and where a story happens. *Chang's Paper Pony* takes place more than one hundred years ago during the California Gold Rush. You find clues to the setting in both the story and the pictures. For example, Chang carries in wood for the stove and water from the

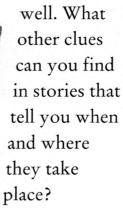

well. What other clues can you find in stories that tell you when and where they take place?

Glossary

an·nounce (ə nouns′), **1** to give public or formal notice of: *The teacher announced that there would be no school tomorrow.* **2** to make known the presence or arrival of: *The loudspeaker announced each airplane as it landed at the airport.* verb, **an·nounc·es, an·nounced, an·nounc·ing.**

an·noy (ə noi′), to make somewhat angry; disturb: *I asked them to turn off the radio because it was annoying me.* verb.

au·di·ence (ô′dē əns), **1** a group of people that sees or hears something: *The audience at the theater enjoyed the play. That movie theater always has a large audience.* **2** a formal interview with a person of high rank: *The ambassador was granted an audience with the queen.* noun.

cage (kāj), **1** a frame or place closed in with wires, iron bars, or wood. *Carla kept the injured squirrel safe in a cage until it could take care of itself.* **2** a thing shaped or used like a cage. Bank tellers or movie cashiers sometimes work in a cage. **3** to put or keep in a cage: *Wild animals should not be caged.* 1,2 noun, 3 verb, **cag·es, caged, cag·ing.**

chick (chik), **1** a young chicken. **2** a young bird: *We watched the robin chicks learning to fly.* noun.

com·fort·a·ble (kum′fər tə bəl), **1** giving comfort: *A soft, warm bed is comfortable.* **2** in comfort; free from pain or hardship: *We felt comfortable in the warm house after a cold day outdoors.* adjective.

con·cerned (kən sėrnd′), **1** troubled; worried; anxious: *The father of the sick child had a concerned look on his face.* **2** interested: *Concerned citizens make use of their right to vote.* adjective.

cage (def. 1)
The parakeet lives in a **cage** indoors.

con·tent (kən tent′), **1** to satisfy; please: *Nothing contents me when I am sick.* **2** satisfied; pleased: *Corrie needs to jog every day in order to be content.* **3** contentment; satisfaction: *The cat lay beside the fire in sleepy content.* 1 verb, 2 adjective, 3 noun.

dis·grace (dis grās′), **1** the loss of honor or respect; shame: *The disgrace of being sent to prison was hard for them to bear.* **2** to cause disgrace to; bring shame upon: *The traitor disgraced his family and friends.* **3** a person or thing that causes dishonor or shame: *My brother's messy room is a disgrace.* 1,3 *noun,* 2 *verb,* **dis·grac·es, dis·graced, dis·grac·ing.**

di·ver·sion (də vėr′zhən), **1** a turning aside: *The thief created a diversion so he could rob the newsstand while no one was looking.* **2** a relief from work or care; amusement; entertainment; pastime. *noun.*

diversion (def. 2)
Playing soccer is a popular **diversion**.

a hat		**i** it		**oi** oil		**ch** child		**ə** stands for:	
ā age		**ī** ice		**ou** out		**ng** long		a in about	
ä far		**o** hot		**u** cup		**sh** she		e in taken	
e lĕt		**ō** open		**ù** put		**th** thin		i in pencil	
ē equal		**ô** order		**ü** rule		**ŦH** then		o in lemon	
ėr term						**zh** measure		u in circus	

draft·y (draf′tē), in a current of air: *The room was drafty, so I closed the window.* *adjective,* **draft·i·er, draft·i·est.**

dread·ful (dred′fəl), **1** causing dread; terrible; fearful: *The fairy tale was about a dreadful monster.* **2** very bad; very unpleasant: *I have a dreadful cold.* *adjective.*

dread·ful·ly (dred′fəl ē), in a dreadful manner: *Mel was dreadfully upset when we were late.* *adverb.* See **dreadful.**

en·e·my (en′ə mē), **1** a person or group that hates or tries to harm another; foe. Two countries fighting against each other are enemies. *The king watched the troops of his enemy approach.* **2** anything that will harm: *Frost is an enemy of flowers.* *noun,* *plural* **en·e·mies.**

ex·haust·ed (eg zô′stid), **1** used up: *The teacher's patience was exhausted by the students' jabbering.* **2** worn out; very tired: *The exhausted hikers stopped to rest after their long walk.* *adjective.*

fade (fād), **1** to become less bright; lose color: *My blue jeans faded after they were washed several times.* **2** to lose freshness or strength; wither: *The flowers in our garden faded at the end of the summer.* **3** to die away; disappear little by little: *The sound of the train faded after it went by. verb,* **fades, fad·ed, fad·ing.**

fierce (firs), **1** savage; wild: *An angry mother bear can be fierce.* **2** very great or strong; intense: *We closed the windows and doors against the fierce wind. adjective,* **fierc·er, fierc·est.**

fierce (def. 1)
The snake looked **fierce.**

fright (frīt), **1** a sudden fear; sudden terror: *The movie monster filled the watchers with fright.* **2** a person or thing that is ugly, shocking, or ridiculous: *When I put on the wig, they laughed and said I looked like a fright. noun.*

fur·i·ous (fyùr′ē əs), **1** very angry; full of wild, fierce anger: *The owner of the house was furious when the neighbor children broke her window playing ball.* **2** raging; violent: *A hurricane is a furious storm. adjective.*

glit·ter (glit′ər), **1** to shine with a bright, sparkling light: *The stars glittered overhead.* **2** a bright, sparkling light: *The glitter of the harsh lights hurt my eyes.* **3** tiny, sparkling objects such as tinsel or spangles, used for decoration. **1** *verb,* **2,3** *noun.*

grace·ful (grās′fəl), **1** beautiful in form or movement: *The audience cheered the graceful skater.* **2** pleasing; agreeable: *a graceful speech of thanks. adjective.*

grum·ble (grum′bəl), **1** to complain in a bad-tempered way; mutter in discontent; find fault: *The students are always grumbling about the food in the cafeteria.* **2** a mutter of discontent; bad-tempered complaint. **3** to make a low, heavy sound like far-off thunder. **1,3** *verb,* **grum·bles, grum·bled, grum·bling; 2** *noun.*

hast·i·ly (hā′stl ē), **1** in a hurried way; quickly and not very carefully: *Abdul glanced hastily at his watch.* **2** rashly: *A decision to change jobs should not be made hastily. adverb.*

heart·y (här′tē), **1** warm and friendly; full of feeling; sincere: *We gave our old friends a hearty welcome.* **2** strong and well; vigorous: *Hearty pioneers moved westward.* **3** with plenty to eat; nourishing: *A hearty meal satisfied her appetite.* adjective, **heart·i·er, heart·i·est.**

hor·ri·ble (hôr′ə bəl), **1** causing horror; frightful; shocking: *a horrible crime, a horrible disease.* **2** extremely unpleasant: *Juan wrinkled up his nose at the horrible smell.* adjective.

hos·pi·tal (hos′pi təl), a place for the care of the sick or injured: *We visited my grandfather in the hospital after his operation.* noun.

in·ten·tion (in ten′shən), a purpose; plan: *Our intention is to visit Yellowstone National Park on our vacation.* noun.

la·goon (lə gün′), a pond or small lake connected with a larger body of water: *Many kinds of birds make their home in that lagoon.* noun.

lagoon

a	hat	i	it	oi	oil	ch	child	ə	stands for:
ā	age	ī	ice	ou	out	ng	long		a in about
ä	far	o	hot	u	cup	sh	she		e in taken
e	let	ō	open	ù	put	th	thin		i in pencil
ē	equal	ô	order	ü	rule	ᵺ	then		o in lemon
ėr	term					zh	measure		u in circus

loos·en (lü′sn), to make or become loose; untie; unfasten: *Joe loosened the ribbon and opened his birthday present.* verb.

nag (nag), to scold; annoy; find fault with all the time: *I will clean up my room if you will stop nagging me. When he was sick he nagged at everybody.* verb, **nags, nagged, nag·ging.**

nerv·ous (nėr′vəs), **1** of the nerves: *a nervous disorder, nervous energy.* **2** easily excited or upset: *A person who has been overworking is likely to become nervous.* **3** restless or uneasy; timid: *Are you nervous about meeting new people?* adjective.

nest (nest), **1** a structure shaped something like a bowl, built by birds out of twigs, leaves, or straw, as a place in which to lay their eggs and protect their young ones: *a robin's nest.* **2** a structure or place used by insects, fishes, turtles, rabbits, or the like, for a similar purpose: *a squirrel's nest, a wasp's nest.* **3** to make and use a nest: *The bluebirds are nesting here now.* 1,2 noun, 3 verb.

re·hears·al (ri hėr′səl), a rehearsing; a practicing to prepare for a public performance: *The teacher said rehearsals for the class play would begin on Wednesday.* noun.

re·mark (ri märk′), **1** to say in a few words; state; comment: *She remarked that it was a beautiful day.* **2** something said in a few words; short statement: *The president of the club made a few remarks.* 1 *verb,* 2 *noun.*

re·spect (ri spekt′), **1** honor; esteem: *The children always showed great respect for their grandparents.* **2** to feel or show honor or esteem for: *We respect an honest person.* **3** care; consideration: *We should show respect for school buildings, parks, and other public property.* 1,3 *noun,* 2 *verb.*

salt (sôlt), **1** a white substance found in the earth and in sea water. Salt is used to season and preserve food: *Don't put too much salt on your food.* **2** containing salt: *The ocean is a great body of salt water.* **3** to season with salt; sprinkle with salt: *We salted the popcorn before eating it.* 1 *noun,* 2 *adjective,* 3 *verb.*
salt away or **salt down, 1** to pack with salt to preserve: *The fish were salted down in a barrel.* **2** to store away: *She is salting away money for her retirement.*

salt·y (sôl′tē), containing salt; tasting of salt. Sweat and tears are salty. *adjective,* **salt·i·er, salt·i·est.**

snick·er (snik′ər), **1** a sly or silly laugh; giggle. **2** to laugh in this way: *The children were snickering to each other.* 1 *noun,* 2 *verb.*

splash·y (splash′ē), **1** making a splash: *The baby likes to play splashy games in her bath.* **2** in a show-off manner: *The actress made a splashy bow to the crowd.* *adjective,* **splash·i·er, splash·i·est.**

stretch (strech), **1** to draw out; extend to full length: *The bird stretched its wings. She stretched herself out on the grass to rest.* **2** to extend one's body or arms and legs: *I stretched out on the couch.* **3** to continue over a distance; extend from one place to another; fill space; spread: *The forest stretches for miles.* verb.

stretch
(def. 2)

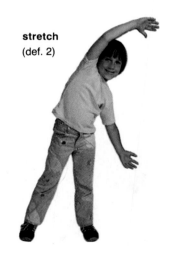

126

sym·pa·thy (sim′pə thē), **1** a sharing of another's sorrow or trouble: *We feel sympathy for a person who is ill.* **2** having the same feeling: *The sympathy between the twins was so great that they always smiled or cried at the same things.* **3** agreement; favor: *I am in sympathy with your plan.* *noun, plural* **sym·pa·thies.**

tease (tēz), **1** to worry by jokes, questions, requests, or the like; annoy: *Carl teased Jackie until she shoved him into a mud puddle.* **2** a person who teases. **1** *verb,* **teas·es, teased, teas·ing; 2** *noun.*

tel·e·graph (tel′ə graf), **1** a way of sending coded messages over wires by means of electricity. **2** a device used for sending these messages: *The man tapped out his message on the telegraph.* **3** to send a message by telegraph: *Mother telegraphed congratulations to the bride and groom.* **1,2** *noun,* **3** *verb.*

temp·ta·tion (temp tā′shən), **1** a tempting: *No temptation could make her break her promise.* **2** a thing that tempts: *Money left carelessly about is a temptation.* *noun.*

un·cer·tain (un sėrt′n), **1** not certain; doubtful: *Hal was uncertain of the directions to Lucia's house.* **2** likely to change; not to be depended on: *Mr. Smith has an uncertain temper.* *adjective.*

a hat	i it	oi oil	ch child	ə stands for:
ā age	ī ice	ou out	ng long	a in about
ä far	o hot	u cup	sh she	e in taken
e let	ō open	ú put	th thin	i in pencil
ē equal	ô order	ü rule	∓H then	o in lemon
ėr term			zh measure	u in circus

va·cant (vā′kənt), **1** not occupied or filled; empty: *The Goldbergs are going to buy that vacant house.* **2** empty of thought or intelligence: *When I asked her a question, she just gave me a vacant smile.* *adjective.*

telegraph
The **telegraph** was the first device to use electricity to send messages.

wish (wish), **1** to have a desire; want: *Do you wish to go home? Sarita wished for a new bicycle.* **2** a desire; need: *I have no wish to be rich. What is your wish?* **3** a saying of something desired: *Please give them my best wishes for a happy New Year.* **1** *verb,* **2,3** *noun, plural* **wish·es.**

Acknowledgments

Text

Pages 6–19: "Lucas Makes a Bet" from *Class Clown* by Johanna Hurwitz. Copyright © 1987 by Johanna Hurwitz. Reprinted by permission of William Morrow and Company, Inc.

Pages 20–22: "A Bug in the Milk" by Johanna Hurwitz. Copyright © 1991 by Johanna Hurwitz.

Pages 24–30: "Louella's Song" by Eloise Greenfield. Copyright © 1975 by Eloise Greenfield. Reprinted by permission of the author.

Pages 32–44: "Priscilla, Meet Felicity" from *Best Enemies* by Kathleen Leverich, illustrations by Susan Condie Lamb. Copyright © 1989 by Kathleen Leverich. Illustrations copyright © 1989 by Susan Condie Lamb. Reprinted by permission of Greenwillow Books, a division of William Morrow & Company, Inc.

Pages 46–62: *Tacky the Penguin* by Helen Lester, illustrated by Lynn Munsinger. Text copyright © 1988 by Helen Lester. Illustrations copyright © 1988 by Lynn Munsinger. Reprinted by permission of Houghton Mifflin Company.

Pages 64–82: *Old Henry* by Joan W. Blos, illustrations by Stephen Gammell. Copyright © 1987 by Joan W. Blos. Illustrations copyright © 1987 by Stephen Gammell. Reprinted by permission of William Morrow and Company, Inc.

Pages 84–93: *Chang's Paper Pony* by Eleanor Coerr. Text copyright © 1988 by Eleanor Coerr. Reprinted by permission of HarperCollins Publishers.

Pages 94–96: "Searching for Gold" by Eleanor Coerr. Copyright © 1991 by Eleanor Coerr.

Pages 98–104: "The Great Flamingo Roundup" from *Ranger Rick*, April 1990, pp. 32–37. Copyright © 1990 by National Wildlife Federation. Reprinted by permission of the publisher, the National Wildlife Federation.

Pages 106–116: *Kate Shelley and the Midnight Express* by Margaret K. Wetterer. Illustrations by Karen Ritz. Copyright © 1990 by Carolrhoda Books, Inc., Minneapolis, MN. Reprinted by permission of the publisher. All rights reserved.

Artists

Illustrations owned and copyrighted by the illustrator.
Lisa Berrett, cover, 1-3
John Weber, calligraphy, 1-3
Steve Snodgrass, 7, 8, 13, 15, 19, 121
Jan Spivey Gilchrist, 24–31
Susan Condie Lamb, 32, 36, 39, 43
Lynn Munsinger, 46–63
Stephen Gammell, 64–83
Byron Gin, 84–93, 97, 121
Karen Ritz, 106–116

Photographs

Unless otherwise acknowledged, all photographs are the property of Scott Foresman.
Page 20: Courtesy of Johanna Hurwitz
Page 94: The New York Historical Society, New York, New York
Page 94 (INS): California Section Picture Collection/California State Library, Sacramento, California
Page 96: Courtesy of Eleanor Coerr
Page 98 (INS): John Cancalosi
Pages 98–99(BG),100–104: C. C. Lockwood/Cactus Clyde Productions
Page 124: D. Lyons/Bruce Coleman, Inc.
Page 125: Don and Pat Valenti
Page 127: Courtesy Deutsches Museum, Munich

Glossary

The contents of the Glossary have been adapted from *Beginning Dictionary*, Copyright © 1988, Scott, Foresman and Company.